Acknowledgements

A big "Thank you" goes out to Jeffrey, Yosemite Park who helped greatly with details about the park.

A big "Thank you" also goes out to Nathan Foster of Terminal Ballistics Research, Taranaki New Zealand. Weaponry.

And a Special "Thank You" goes out to Dianne, my best critic and cheerleader.

Mike Murphy Park Ranger

The Bear

"Good morning Gladys," said Mike Murphy as he took off his park ranger jacket, put it on a coat hook, then hung it up on a rack behind the door. Gladys was wearing a white, no collar, buttoned to the top, blouse and black slacks that morning. She wore dark rimmed glasses and very little make-up underneath the auburn hair that fell straight down to her shoulders, ending in a few curls. Her smile was quick and genuine as she looked up from her typewriter and asked "And a very good morning to you Mike. That was a short two week honeymoon, everything okay?" "Yes, everything is fine. Alanah decided to return to the campus and finish up on her masters. We talked it over and agreed to commute every other weekend until she graduates. After that she hopes to join the staff here." "Sounds reasonable. We are short staffed as it is. You think I should talk to the boss or would you prefer to handle it?" "Thanks for the offer Gladys but when the time comes I'll let you know about some face time with Mr. Summers." "Sounds like a plan. If you want to catch up on things check the bulletin board. Hasn't been much excitement, which is a little unusual considering it's a new season." "Will do," agreed Mike as he turned, walked down a short narrow hallway and stood in front of a large brown peg board laden with post it notes and sheets of paper held down by colored thumb tacks.

Mike's back was turned and he did not see his boss come up behind him and start to pour himself a cup of hot coffee from the small aluminum pot sitting on a hot plate. "Morning Mike, back from the honeymoon already? Trouble?" asked Mr. Summers. Startled, Mike jumped slightly, then turned, smiled and said, "Morning Ryan, boss, no, things are great. As I mentioned to Gladys when I checked in, Alanah decided to return to the campus and finish up her masters then put in for a position here. I understand we are a little short handed? Last season we were fully staffed. I realize we had a very busy year and record visitors but we've had hectic schedules before. What happened?"

"Let's go to my office and talk," suggested Mr. Summers as he took a white napkin and wrapped it around two glazed donuts. "Had a short night," he explained. Mike poured himself a cup of coffee, added a little vanilla creamer, followed Ryan to his office and then sat down across the desk from him. " You mentioned Alanah maybe putting in for a position here? As a ranger or office staff?" "She wasn't specific when we talked on the way to the airport last Friday but my guess would be as a ranger. She's a natural. Not once did she complain about living out of a tent the whole two weeks of our honeymoon. She even suggested it. In fact, she was up before I was most of the time getting the fire going and breakfast started." "We could definitely use the help. Let her know she has a place with us, whenever she is ready. On a personal note, Mike, how are you doing with handling the experience up at the Ostrander a few years ago?"

"Just fine Chief. Part of the job. True, it was just a

skiing accident which happens sometimes when you mix alcohol and young people. Driving the big snow-cat wasn't a problem. But that's not the reason you wanted to talk, is it?" "No, it isn't Mike. The reason is I will be taking a leave of absence, starting next Monday. There is a family illness that I must take care of. Without going into great detail I'll just say the doctor's visit for Barbara did not go well, but that doesn't leave the room. I will arrange a staff meeting later this morning and inform everyone about leaving, but I wanted to let you know first and ask if you would go the extra mile with helping to keep things under control. I realize you aren't the senior ranger, but I have learned to trust your instincts over the years." "Yes, Sir, Chief. Thank you for the vote of confidence and I'll do my best and hope things turn out with the family." Glancing down at the watch on his wrist, Mike said," Mr. Summers, if you have nothing further , I am behind on my morning run and I saw a note on the board about some visitors up on the Merced who are messy campers." "It's a new season Mike, welcome back." "Thanks Chief, I'll get a vehicle from Gladys on my way out. Rising from his chair Mike extended his hand across the desk and the two of them shook hands.

After leaving the boss's office, Mike returned to the bulletin board and found the notice about the messy campers. According to the location he guessed it to be about a mile downstream from where he and Alanah had spent their honeymoon. Taking a note pad and pen from his shirt pocket, he copied down the information, clicked the pen with his thumb, then returned them to the pocket. *Time to get started,* he said to himself. At the reception desk, he stopped and asked Gladys if the wrangler was gassed up? With a smile she answered and said, "Of course Mike, always. You are the only one who likes to drive it. The other rangers prefer larger vehicles with air conditioning in the summer months." "The wrangler has a heater," said Mike. "Yes, but not AC. I guess they aren't as tough as you, "said Gladys as she smiled broadly and chuckled. "You know where the keys are and you have your gas card, right?" "Yes, Ma-am. I'll check out that messy camper notice on the Merced and call in when I get there." "Thanks Mike and welcome back."

After retrieving his jacket from the coat rack Mike slipped it over his shoulders and was thankful for its comforting warmth when he opened the front door to go outside. It was the last day of May and the air still had a little bite in it left over from the winter. There was virtually no wind and the sun was already half way up the sky. He guessed the temperature to be around forty which was normal for that time of year. He reached into an inside pocket of his jacket, found his gloves and sunglasses and put them on. As Mike walked the short distance to the motor pool he heard the sound of an impatient driver honking the horn on their vehicle. He turned and spotted a black pickup sitting behind a line of other cars waiting to get started on their vacation. Mike raised his glasses to better observe the driver and watched as he raised his arm out the truck window and motion for the drivers in front of him to move forward. The driver then honked the horn again and then toss his still burning cigarette out the window onto the parking lot. Taking a deep breath and slowly letting it out, Mike walked over and stood beside the window of the truck.

The driver was taking a drink from a water bottle and turned to face Mike. "You got a problem?" "Yes, I do," answered Mike. "I just observed you tossing a burning cigarette out the window of your vehicle. I am going to give you a verbal warning and remind you of the danger of forest fires." "Do you see any forests here in the parking lot? It's all cement and asphalt," asked the driver. His voice was very agitated. As Mike stood there and talked to the driver, he caught the familiar odor of alcohol. He couldn't smell any on the driver's breath, but he knew there was probably some in the vehicle. The driver was unshaven with what looked to be a four day old beard. He had on a red and yellow, flannel checkered shirt and a tan colored, sheep's wool lined jacket. He looked like someone familiar with being in the outdoors.

"Are you planning on camping out in the park?" asked Mike. "Yeah, I've got a four day permit, if I ever get there." "I hope you use some caution when you get to your campsite concerning open fires. Fires and alcohol are sometimes a bad combination, if you get my drift?" "Yeah, yeah, I got the message," said the driver as he shook his head and then closed the window, leaving Mike standing on the black asphalt. The line of vehicles slowly moved forward and as the truck passed Mike he looked at the truck's license plate and mentally wrote it down. He also noticed several places around the vehicle's wheel wells and rear bumper, black tape had been applied in an attempt to hide rust spots. "Have a good day," said Mike as the truck exited the parking lot.

Looking down at the pavement between his feet Mike saw the still smoldering cigarette. Taking his right thick soled boot, he ground out the butt, reached down, picked it up and then deposited it into one of the cigarette butt stands on the curb next to the roadside. From where he was standing the jeep wrangler was parked in one of the spaces reserved for staff members. As he seated himself in the driver's seat of the vehicle Mike took a few seconds to breathe deeply to relax before turning the key and starting the engine. The wrangler had a standard transmission and with practiced ease, he engaged the clutch and ten minutes later he was on the road, leaving the ranger station to disappear in his rearview mirror and thirty minutes after that he pulled off the road into a two-car parking space. From there it was only twenty yards to the river and where the messy campers had been reported. Arriving at the campsite, he looked upstream and shook his head, he had been right in his estimation; it was almost exactly two miles from where he and Alanah had spent their honeymoon.

Looking around, he saw empty beer bottles, crumpled paper, a few small dark brown cardboard boxes and many small pieces of paper blowing around on the ground. Over by the rack where the heavy, bear-proof trash cans and dumpster sat were several large, black, contractor sized, plastic bags, stuffed and overflowing with garbage. Even being upwind Mike could still smell the thick rank odor. *This would take a clean up crew most of the day to get it ready for the next park guest.* "Well, better call it in," said Mike as he started picking up a few bottles and beer cans on his way to the jeep and its radio.

As he sat behind the wheel he reached over to the radio and taking the mike in one hand, brought it up to his mouth and pressed the button. "Mike to base." After several seconds and not hearing an acknowledgment, he called again. Finally the familiar voice of Gladys came back over the speaker. "Base to Mike. What do you need?" "Gladys? I thought Louise was on duty today?" "She was for about an hour and then had to go home. Morning sickness. You know? I'm doing double duty. What's up?" "I'm here at the messy campers site and a mess would be an understatement. Can you send up a crew? I'll stick around and get started until they arrive. As long as I have your ear can you run a check on a license plate for me?" "Sure thing Mike, hang on." It took less than a minute before the radio crackled to life and Gladys informed him it was a Silverado pickup and belonged to a man from upstate New York.

The pieces fit the description of the vehicle he had seen earlier in the parking lot and the rust spots indicated the truck had been exposed to many trips in the snow on salt laden roads. "Thanks Gladys. About how long before the cleaning crew gets here?" "With the traffic conditions, no sooner than an hour, Mike, sorry." "Don't apologize, it isn't your fault. I'll get started and do what I can. If it takes a while to get it ready I might as well camp out for the night and get an early start in the morning." "Thanks Mike and I'll put a burr under their saddles."

A Burr under their saddles indeed, Mike thought to himself as he hung the radio mike on its familiar hook on the dashboard. Gladys had been a farm girl from Wisconsin and had been raised around horses and milk cows. By her using the saddle burr term he knew she meant she would expedite the cleaning crew on their way. Forty-five minutes later a fifteen passenger van and a medium sized dump truck arrived and eight people got out of the van. They all wore light brown, one piece jump suits that zipped up in the front. Mike walked over and greeted them. "Anybody bring pizza?' he asked. "Pizza? Are you kidding? It looks like someone has already had a serious party here," said a guy wearing a hard hat. "Okay gang, let's get started. This job is a big one and we will earn our pay today, for sure.

It took the better part of the day to close the last garbage bag and toss it into the bed of the dump truck. The campsite was ready for the next park visitor. As the clean up crew piled back into the van to leave, Mike shook the man in charge's hand and said, "Thanks guys. I will fill out a written report when I get back to base in the morning. I hate to see anyone get barred from the park, but I think this time an exception will be made.

An hour and a half later, Mike sat on an old log at the site's fire-pit and extended his hands out over the fire to warm them. Technically open fires weren't allowed in the park until June, which was tomorrow. He glanced at his wrist watch, which was clearly visible in the light of a full moon. The watche's hands read 12:15. Mike liked rules and regulations as they kept things neat and orderly. He was tired and yawned several times. The day's warmth had quickly vanished almost as soon as the sun went down. His breath frosted slightly in the evening air. As Mike sat there he gazed into the fire and smiled as he remembered other evenings around campfires in his younger days. He looked up and saw myriads of stars twinkling in the dark sky, like diamonds on black velvet. Off in the distance a wolf lifted his voice to serenade the full moon.

After pouring two buckets of cold river water over the fire he put his hand over the ashes and felt no heat. Then he went around the campsite and gathered a few small sticks and kindling for the morning fire and stacked them neatly beside the fire-pit. He yawned a few more times, which told him his body was in the process of shutting down for the day.

Earlier, he had unpacked his camping gear from the jeep and laid out his sleeping bag about five feet from the unlit fireplace. As he removed his boots he was careful to turn them upside down on small wooden stakes beside the sleeping bag. This was an old trick to help keep insects and other small critters out, plus give the boots a chance to air out. Then he laid down on the sleeping bag and pulled its warm flap up around his chin and settled his head onto a firm pillow. The pillow was one concession he allowed himself when he slept out under the stars. Down by the river, frogs croaked and sent their messages, stating they were happy and glad to be alive. Within fifteen minutes Mike was sound asleep. Sometime during the night the evening's concert was joined by the soft chirring made by a four-footed, masked visitor as he busily washed his evening meal of crawfish in the river.

The next morning he found tracks along the river bank which had not been there before he turned in for the night. Looking down at the tracks he could see they were from a bear and a fairly large one, as he guessed them to be almost five inches across.

Chapter Two

After drawing a small bucket of water from the river Mike poured it into an aluminum basin and proceeded to wash his face and brush his teeth. It was just barely sunrise and the temperature was already pushing forty degrees. As he looked into the side mirror of the jeep Mike lathered up a bar of soap and spread it onto his jaws and cheeks. Just as he pulled at the skin below his jaw line and make the first stroke with a safety razor static came over the jeep's radio followed by a young voice. "Base to Mike?" He laid the razor down, wiped his hand clear from soap and picked up the radio mike.

"Good morning Louise. Hope you're feeling better." "Yes, thank you. I was so embarrassed yesterday morning." "Quite understandable and congratulations." "It was an uneventful evening and night here after the cleanup crew finished and left. You didn't call this early to just say morning, what's up?" "Late yesterday afternoon a call came in about a large bear sighting over by the Tuolumne visitor center. Can you check it out?" "Can do, no problem," said Mike as he glanced at his wrist watch." Over by Tuolumne you say? That's about ten miles from my location. It's seven-thirty now. Will call back, say around eight-thirty or nine?" "Thanks Mike. Base out."

Breakfast would have to wait, he decided. A bear sighting was normal at any given time in the Spring when females came out of hibernation and most of them had at least one cub with them. There had never been a fatal bear attack in the history of the park, as far as he knew anyway, but there was always the exception if a guest was careless. Mike quickly gathered up his camping gear and stowed it away in the Jeep. Taking a last look around the campsite to make sure he had not forgotten anything, he climbed into the passenger seat and was on his way. During his five year tenure at the park he had traveled over every road and trail at least once and that morning he wasted no time getting to the visitor center at Tuolumne.

The air was exceptionally clean that morning and during the ride he took several deep breaths, taking in all the scents nature had to offer. There wasn't any wood smoke from campfires, yet and that was a little unusual considering it was still early morning and guests were cooking breakfast. At the thought of food his stomach rumbled loudly reminding him he had not had any yet. He kept his speed down to around twenty-five miles an hour, which would give him plenty of time to stop and avoid hitting any animals.

As he drove, Mike kept both hands on the wheel, but draped his left elbow on the window sill. It was a comfortable position which allowed him to drive and be observant at the same time. During the time it took to get to Tuolumne, which was about thirty minutes he did not see a single animal along the route. At the visitors center he checked in and the dispatcher informed him about the bear sighting. It had been a female with two cubs. A man had called it in who was vacationing with his wife and son. They had observed proper protocol and the bear had

12

not approached closer than thirty yards from them. The man also mentioned that during the previous night there had not been any sounds of crickets or frogs. Mike wrote down the location, given by the dispatcher, on his notepad and in ten minutes he drove into the parking space at their campsite.

His boots crunched lightly on the gravel as he walked the short distance and announced himself to a man sitting on a folding chair beside a small fire. "Good morning Sir, Mike Murphy, park ranger. I understand you saw a bear and cubs yesterday morning?" The man stood up and extended his hand. "John Saxon. Yes, my wife, myself and our son were hiking and the bear came out of the underbrush with her cubs. I remembered the instructions given by the receptionist when we checked in and whispered them to Susan and Joseph. She did not charge and then just disappeared back into the forest." "I understand the incident took place about fifty yards from your camp?" asked Mike. "Correct. The trail we were on is right behind our tent over there," said John as he motioned with his hand, " Take a right until you come to a small clearing. Just on the other side is some underbrush. Can't miss it." "Thanks Mr. Saxon. Please have a pleasant and hopefully uneventful, vacation here at Yosemite." The two of them again shook hands.

It didn't take but a few minutes for Mike to follow the directions and he found himself standing at the edge of a small clearing. Across from him, about fifteen yards away, he saw the clump of underbrush described by John. He looked down at the dirt at his feet for any

13

tracks and seeing none proceeded slowly across the clearing. The air was strangely still as he walked, keeping his senses on high alert. In all probability, the bear and her cubs were long gone in search for food, but caution was always a good thing.

Arriving at the underbrush Mike looked around and easily spotted the familiar tracks of a bear and two sets of small ones, which would be the cubs. Taking a small tape measure from his jacket pocket, he knelt and measured one of the larger tracks. Using a rough formula of one inch to a foot, he guessed the female to be about five feet. *Typical,* he thought to himself. As Mike turned to go back to the camp, he saw a cluster of bear droppings off to the side of the trail, almost hidden by fallen leaves. It wasn't the deposit itself that raised his curiosity, it was the size of some of the individual nuggets; they were almost three inches across! He quickly looked around the area for any tracks, but the ground was too hard and left no trace.

Mike wasted no time and quickly walked back to the Saxon campsite and found the family sitting around the fire eating breakfast. As he approached them, he could smell freshly cooked bacon. Again, his stomach rumbled ominously to remind him he had not eaten yet. " Mr. Saxon, you have a minute, please?" Mike asked as he walked a few steps to the side. "Of course," John answered and then asked, "Did you find the place?" "Yes, excellent directions. Thank you. I don't want to cause any alarm, but while I was checking out the spot I also found signs of a fairly large bear. I don't know if it is male or female as yet, but precautions should be taken and keep alert." "Thanks for the heads up, Mr. Murphy. It's been a fantastic vacation. This is the last day and we'll be heading back to Oklahoma this afternoon."

A sense of urgency was in Mike's thoughts on the way back to the office as he sat behind the wheel of the Wrangler. There had always been reports of bears raiding trash barrels in the park. No matter how informed the guests said they were, it never failed that close encounters always happened. Some bears had become accustomed to eating human food and would sometimes go to great lengths to get it; even to the point of breaking the windows of vehicles if they smelled food inside.

The Saxon bear sighting had been slightly Northeast of the Tuolumne Visitor Center, roughly twenty miles from the Valley Visitor Center. Mike called in to the office and made his report. He felt this was a special case because of the evidence left behind by the mystery bear. Without knowing if the bear was male or female, he could only rely on his training and gut instinct which added up to the animal being a female. In less than an hour, Mike drove the Wrangler to the White Wolf lodge, turned off the key and put it into his jacket pocket. Virtually every parking spot in the lot was occupied by a vehicle and more were waiting to park when a vacancy opened up. *It was going to be another very busy season,* Mike told himself as he quickly walked the short distance to the front door .He was hungry and the White Wolf featured an excellent breakfast buffet.

It didn't take but a few minutes for Mike to go through

the line and select his breakfast items, then find a vacant seat. Breakfast was the best part of the day and it didn't matter if it was seven in the morning or ten at night. As he looked down at his plate, he realized he did not get any syrup for the hotcakes. He glanced at the long line of guests at the buffet table and decided to use the jelly packets that were on a small tray by the table. He selected two strawberry packets and after spreading them on the hotcakes, he cut a small section off with his fork and ate it. *Hmm, not bad,* he told himself as he continued to eat, bacon, scrambled eggs and drink hot, fresh, black coffee.

Thirty minutes later he paid the bill for the meal and was sitting behind the wheel of the Wrangler. "Base to Mike," The radio squawked. "Mike to base, what's up?" "Traffic is already starting to build up over at Valley Center. Can you head over there and help out?" "Can do Louise, no problem."

For the rest of the day and into late afternoon Mike was kept very busy directing traffic and settling a minor squabble when two people wanted the same parking spot. He was one tired man when six PM rolled around and the traffic finally slowed to a trickle. During the day Mike had a chance to observe two other rangers who were on traffic duty. Ruth and Stephanie were relatively new at the park and had come on board two years ago. They were in their late twenties and single. Ruth was from Texas and Stephanie from Montana. A few times he had watched as they worked together to handle pedestrians, both going to and coming from the Center.

They were both dressed in summer field uniforms; olive drab , short sleeve shirts with the arrowhead emblem over the left side pocket and name tag over the right side pocket, neatly pressed ,forest green pants and a light brown, breezer work hat. They looked very professional.

When the traffic had finally dwindled down and could manage on its own, the two rangers came over and introduced themselves. Mike already knew their names, but accepted theirs and introduced himself. Ruth seemed to be a natural around people and said," Thank you Mike for saving the day. We would have been in deep trouble otherwise. " "No problem ladies, glad to have helped, but you seemed to work well together and handle yourselves very professionally." The two of them looked at each other then Stephanie said, "Well, as it turns out we are both farm girls and used to hard work. Cars and trucks aren't the same as cows and sheep so you have to use a little more patience. Will you be here tomorrow?" "Don't know," Mike answered." Normally Tuesday is my day to make the rounds to primitive campsites but I'll ask when I call in to the office in the morning. Deal?" "Deal," said both of them together.

Chapter Three

The sound of birds woke Mike up from a sound sleep. Turning back the flap on the sleeping bag he looked at his wrist watch; six-thirty and the sun was already half way up."Well, time to rise and shine and meet the day," said Mike as he reached out, found the zipper and opened the bag. The morning air smelled fresh and clean with pine and as he took a deep breath there was a faint odor of wood smoke. The spot he had camped at for the evening was one he often used. There were many campsites with tents he could have chosen from but this particular spot on the Merced was very close to where guests had reported seeing a large sized trout. Mike always used catch and release if he fished but the idea of trying to catch this one just didn't occur to him. He couldn't always keep an eye on this particular spot to try and keep guests from catching the trout, have it stuffed and hang on a wall somewhere but he could try.

With a little over seven hundred miles of rivers and streams the park was rich with both rainbow and brown trout. The current American record for brown trout had been set in 2009, weighing forty-one pounds, seven ounces and measuring forty-three and a half inches long. Mike did not know the size of the one that had been seen on the Merced but according to the guest it was very large and he intended to try and keep it in Yosemite.

Breakfast that morning was simple, bacon, eggs, sliced potatoes and black coffee, cooked over an open fire. After the meal he freshened up; only using a half gallon of water to brush his teeth, wash his face and upper body. From where he was standing, his view of the river and Bunnell Point was spectacular! The sun was peeking from behind a few clouds and the sky was awash with vibrant colors of light red, orange and pale yellow. How can people say there is no God when all they have to do is be in the forest when it is waking up and see a sunrise like this one? Before he had turned in for the evening Mike had called into the office, made his report and asked if any new details had come in? Louise had informed him there had been nothing out of the ordinary, so Mike said he would check out some sites over at Tamarack Flat.

From his camping spot to where he had parked the jeep, a little off the road at the Visitor Center was about a mile. After storing everything away in the backpack Mike walked the short distance, put the backpack in the rear compartment of the jeep, sat in the front seat and turned the ignition.

Normally Tamarack wasn't open until late May or June but he wanted to check it out anyway before the season opened. It was about twelve miles from Mike's campsite and only took about a half hour to get there. Just as he rounded a curve in the road, he heard music coming from loudspeakers; it was hard rock and the sound of it disturbing a perfectly quiet morning, aggravated Mike. According to the regulations there shouldn't be anyone camping here yet. There were only a few parking spots and those were filled by a black pickup truck and two other suv's. It was the same truck he had seen earlier at the Visitor Center.

Mike parked his vehicle behind the black truck and one of the utility vehicles, partially blocking them in. As he sat in the jeep he looked around the camp and was surprised how clean it looked. Somehow he was expecting waste and garbage everywhere, especially around the trash barrel area. What did bother him however, was someone walking around with a metal detector. Reaching over to the jeep's glove compartment he took out his citation log book just in case, and in less than a minute he was standing in front of the man holding the detector in one hand and a headset with the other. Mike recognized him as the truck driver. "That's in violation of park rules," stated Mike flatly as he pointed to the metal detector. Then he added, "This area isn't open until later in the season."

"What?" asked the man as he removed the headset from his ears. "Metal detectors aren't allowed in the park." "My permit says I can use it if I don't dig anything up without authorization," said the man as he reached into his shirt pocket and produced a piece of paper. Technically the man was right. Mike reached out, took the paper and read its contents. His permit was for five days and allowed the use of metal detectors, but the permit was for an area west of where they were. Mike knew the man was partially correct, but his attitude just didn't exactly set right. "What are you searching for?" "Gold, of course." Mike knew of several places in the rivers and streams around the park where you could pan for gold but anything inside the park was unknown to him. He did not like it when visitors knew more about the park than he did. "I'll have to check on that. Your permit is for a camp west of here. In the meantime, you can continue using the detector in keeping with the rules regarding digging. This is day five of your permit. If you want to extend it you will have to come by a Visitor Center and sign up again."

The man looked at Mike, shrugged his head in acknowledgment and said," Thanks. I guess we got off on the wrong foot. The name's Danielson, Frank Danielson. My buddies and I are from upstate New York on vacation. We're in marketing with a chemical company and none of us have really been camping so we decided to see what it is like." Mike's instincts told him the man wasn't exactly telling the whole truth." As I said earlier about fires, they do no one any good, especially animals. Please use caution." The man didn't offer to shake hands so Mike didn't offer his either and said, "Have a good day," as he turned and left.

His original impression of Danielson had been that of a rude, impatient male having a bad day. His clothing indicated someone accustomed to dressing in layers against the cold and his beard didn't look like someone who worked in a public office. Well, so far they had not violated any park regulations and kept an orderly camp so all Mike could do was file it away in his memory, take a deep breath and get on with making his rounds.

After leaving the Danielson camp Mike pulled off to the side of the road and called in. "Mike to base?" "Base to Mike," came a friendly response, "What's up?"

21

"Louise, I just cautioned a guest up at Tamarack about using a metal detector. That area isn't open yet. I didn't write up a citation, even though they were in the wrong area according to their permit. The guest is Frank Danielson. According to park regulations he can use the detector so I cautioned him about being at the wrong camp and the use of open fires. There were two other vehicles at the campsite; a Honda suv and a Ford Bronco." "Thanks Mike for the update. So far the morning has been smooth and uneventful. Surprisingly the traffic hasn't been a problem, leaving everyone free to attend to other duties. Mr. Summers announced in the meeting he would be taking a short leave of absence, leaving the senior ranger, Jack Stapleton in charge. Otherwise, nothing special for you." "Thanks Louise, Mike out."

It was still early afternoon, so he decided to take a roundabout route back to The Valley Center, grab a good meal, a nice hot bath and turn in for the evening. He liked the outdoors and sleeping under the stars, but a hot bath was always welcome. Many times, if he was in the field ,he would just use a small amount of water from a nearby stream and freshen up the next morning. From his campsite, he decided to take a small road; not much bigger than a game trail, that was more or less a direct route back to The Center and a hot bath.

About half-way there he had to stop and clear away some small tree limbs that had fallen during a storm. It was late afternoon and usually there were already sounds of crickets and frogs, but an eerie silence was all he could hear. He quietly laid down the limb he was holding and slowly stood upright; his senses were on full alert. He sniffed the air for some indication of what might be wrong, but it only smelled of damp earth and pine. Not moving an inch from where he was, Mike began a systematic examination of his surroundings. Nothing out of the ordinary immediately caught his eye, but as he narrowed his focus he saw two small animals on the road about ten feet in front of him.

Taking a few steps forward, Mike stopped. The animals did not move and he saw they were frogs. Finally, Mike stood right beside the frogs and they still did not move or jump away. Something was wrong. The light was not that good in the woods as it was late afternoon, but Mike could easily identify the animals as Yosemite Toads and they were dead.

Ordinarily, Yosemite Toads were found up around the Tuolumne and Tioga Pass area. The one thing that really bothered Mike was that particular species of toads were on the endangered list and to find two of them this far out of their area and dead was far from ordinary. Rather than radio in what he found Mike decided to personally turn in the report at the office and fifteen minutes later he stood in front of Gladys's desk.

Her brow furrowed, Gladys asked," I thought you were done for the day?" "You know how it is with us work-a-holics, our day is never done," said Mike as he chuckled. "Seriously though, as I was taking the scenic route back, I found two Anaxyrus Canorus dead on the road." "Two what Mike?" "Anaxyrus, uh, Yosemite

Toads. They were not smashed as if they had been run over by a vehicle but just sitting there. Normally that species is found up around Tioga Pass, so my question is why were they in that particular area?"

"Sorry Mike, I don't have an answer for you. Yosemite Toads I am familiar with but not under that name. Guess I need to do my homework. I'll pass the information up the ladder for them to decide if any action is warranted." "Works for me. Thanks Gladys. If you have nothing more for me, I think I'll get a good meal and a hot bath. See you in the morning." "Oh, Mike, I almost forgot. About a half hour ago a guest reported a bear sighting up at Backpacker's Camp. According to the report the bear was a big one."

"Gladys, we pretty well know what a big bear looks like, but to a guest it could just be a bear standing upright. A male can be around six feet so to a five-foot six guest, it would be a large bear. Anyway, thanks for the heads-up and I'll check it out in the morning, first thing after breakfast and call in." "Sounds good Mike, have a good evening."

Chapter Four

Morning came and Mike turned over one more time so he could see the alarm clock sitting on the bedside table. He always had an uncanny habit of waking up at the time he mentally set the night before and this morning was no exception; the clock read 5: 55 which meant he had five more minutes of sleep. Closing his eyes, he drifted off into what is known as combat sleep where you are fully awake, but your eyes are closed and you are aware of everything around you. Five minutes later he threw back the warm covers and sat on the edge of the bed. He yawned and stretched his arms over his head. "Well, time to get the day started," he said to no one in particular.

The floor was slightly cool as he walked barefoot to the bathroom to begin his morning routine. Even though he was at The Valley Center, where water was convenient he saw no reason to waste it in taking a long shower. The term 'Navy Shower' came from a procedural to conserve water aboard ships at sea and consisted of quickly rinsing down, turning the water off, soaping and then rinsing off. The time involved was usually around six to eight minutes and only using five gallons or less. Feeling clean and refreshed, he went downstairs to find some breakfast and a cup of hot coffee. A half hour later he was driving out of his parking spot and on the road. According to what Gladys had said the previous evening there had been two bear sightings at Backpackers Camp, about ten miles away. Backpacker's was close to the

West entrance of the park and was well named with roughly ninety-five percent of Yosemite being declared as wilderness. There weren't any designated parking spots at Backpacker's and you had to park a short distance away and walk in. After parking the jeep Mike walked until he smelled bacon and then just followed his nose. Arriving at a campsite he saw two adults sitting at a small four foot square table, with a cup sitting in front of them and they both were holding books. Mike inquired," The Franklin party?" The man looked up from behind his sunglasses and answered, "Yes, Sir, Tobias, Betty and our three sons over by the fire, left to right, Joseph, Aaron and David." Mike Murphy, Yosemite Park Ranger. I understand you had a bear sighting yesterday?"

"Actually, the boys saw the bear while hiking, just before breakfast. They ran back to camp and I called it in. They are all three Life Scouts and working on their Eagle merit badges. My better half, Betty convinced me we need a vacation so to help the boys earn a few badges we decided on Yosemite.

As they sat and chatted, Tobias talked about his family as having solid, Christian beliefs. Early in their marriage, they had decided to home school their children as neither of them liked what was being taught in public schools and discipline was often a foreign word. His wife had Bachelor's degrees in both biology and chemistry and he had a Master's in Business Management.

Tobias went on to explain he was a policeman from L.A. and a Sergeant. "I can call the boys over if you

26

want to talk to them about the bear?" Tobias asked. Mike looked over to where the three were sitting on logs
around a small fire. They each had a plate of food sitting on their knees and were busy eating. "Thanks, but I think I'll go over and join them. After we finish I'll chat a little more with you, if that's okay?" "Sounds like a plan." "Good morning gentlemen," said Mike as he stood by the boys. "Good morning ,Sir," they said in unison. "May I sit down?" " asked Mike as he motioned with his hand towards an unoccupied log across from them. "Sure," answered Joseph. As he sat down Mike introduced himself and asked, "I understand you had a bear sighting yesterday? Can you describe it, Aaron?" "Yes Sir. We were taking our morning hike, right after sunrise and she just appeared on the trail in front of us. She didn't bluff charge and passed by us about five yards away. We observed the rule of standing still around bears." "Any tracks to indicate size, David?" "None that we saw on the trail as the ground was too hard, but the day before Josh, uh, Joshua discovered some along a small creek bank in the mud." "Joshua?" "Yes, Sir. There were a pair of tracks, zigzag fashion. One pair was slightly smaller than the other, possibly a cub, but we didn't actually see any and the smaller tracks didn't look as fresh as the big ones. The larger tracks were about four and a half inches across. Using the formula of one equals one plus one, the bear would probably stand five or six feet." "Aaron, you said she, earlier. You didn't see any cubs so how did you know and please explain using the formula ?" "Well, Mr. Murphy as the bear passed by

us we had a clear view of its rump and there was nothing to indicate it as being a male. The formula is one inch equals one foot and add a foot."

Mike chuckled at Aaron's observation and said," Very good gentlemen, accurate descriptions and detailed information. Your father mentioned something about some merit badges to become Eagle Scouts? What's the boy scout motto?" "Be prepared," came the immediate response from all three. Backpacking is one of the merit badges for Eagle. You like camping out so tell me about preparing your packs, David?" "That one's easy," David answered as he smiled, then continued," FISHFRINN or first-aid, insulation, sunscreen, hydration, fire, repair-kit, illumination, navigation and nutrition." Mike mentally checked off the items on David's list and shook his head in approval. " Well, gentlemen, you know your stuff. Thank you for your time and I hope the remainder of your vacation is filled with having a good time" "You're welcome," said Joseph, "So far it has been awesome!"

As they sat and chatted about hiking, backpacking and being outdoors, Mike looked at the young men sitting across from him and it was almost like seeing carbon copies; they all had clean-cut blond hair, light brown eyes, a few freckles and deep sun tans. Then the four of them stood up and shook hands.

"Mr. Franklin, Betty," said Mike as he approached them at the table. "You have raised your sons well, congratulations." "Thank you Mr. Murphy, said Betty. "We have tried to instill in all of them to be courteous at all times and conscious of other people's feelings. Even being young adults they aren't interested in drugs or alcohol, however, that being said, last year they began to notice girls and going on modified dates together. Before we allowed them to leave the house one of us would talk to the girl to find out their values and what they expected from the date. Most of them also came from Christian families so we felt relatively safe that everything would be fine and so far there hasn't been any exceptions."

"Excellent principles," agreed Mike. "It is refreshing to hear young people express themselves with confidence and not use slang words or vulgarity. Mr. Tobias, if you know your son's troop number and council, I can forward a letter of recognition and recommendation stating I think they are ready for their backpacking and camping merit badges." Thank you, Mr. Murphy, they would appreciate that." Then Mike shook both Tobias's and Betty's hands and said," Have a good day and enjoy the park."

As Mike sat in the jeep driver's seat he took a last look around the camp and an idle thought crossed his mind; Mr. Franklin was wearing a lightweight jacket over a loose fitting shirt and long trousers, was he wearing an under the arm shoulder holster and gun?

Alanah and he had talked about having children, but she wanted to wait until she finished her degree. That way she could devote all her time to raising them properly until they were nine or ten and then employ a nanny. Mike had agreed it was a good plan and as he sat there he shook his head and could only hope they turned out as well mannered as the Franklin children.

The second bear sighting was less than a ten minute drive from the Franklin camp at McGurk Meadow. The caller had said he was hiking and the bear charged him, then disappeared off into the trees. There was a small wooden bridge near where the incident took place. When Gladys had informed him about the two reports, yesterday afternoon, she mentioned the second caller had an English or European accent and sounded very cultured. Mike's main concern was the caller had used the term, charged. Usually bears bluff charged and stopped a few feet away, then retreated or pass at a safe distance. There had never been a fatality concerning bears and guests at the park and he made a concerted effort to see that if it did happen, it would not be on his watch.

At The Meadow Mike quickly located the area described by the caller and the wooden bridge across the stream. It had not rained in a few days, but the dirt and mud along the stream bed was still soft and the tracks were clearly defined and led off in an easterly direction. Kneeling beside the tracks Mike reached into an inside jacket pocket and produced a small, metal encased tape measure.

As he stretched the tape across the prints he measured four and three quarter inches. Using quick math he calculated the bear stood between five and six feet. He wondered if this could be the same bear seen by the Franklin boys, the one reported at the Saxon camp and the tracks he had seen Monday morning? If that were the case the bear was ranging pretty much in the Northern parts of the park and according to the Franklin boys it was a female without cubs. Mike decided he had better call it in.

"Mike to base?" "Yes, Mike. Good morning. Did you check out the bear sightings at Backpackers and McGurk's?" "Yes, Gladys and a good morning to you too. Louise out again?" "No, actually she's in the restroom and I'm holding down the fort." "Both sightings appear to be of the same bear," said Mike. "Probably a female without cubs and a big one." "As in, how big Mike?" "Five maybe six feet." The pause at the other end of the radio told him Gladys was digesting the information she had just heard.

"Wow! That is big, for a female anyway. None of the ones we captured and tagged with GPS were anywhere near that large. A few males, yes. You want to put out an alert?" "Yes, Gladys, please and while you are at it, pass along I would like to try to capture and tag her." "Will do Mike. Are you coming in tonight or staying out?" "Will most likely stay out. The weather has warmed up a little and the night sky is just gorgeous with constellations. Two nights ago was a hunter's moon and you could easily navigate by its light, if you chose to after dark, of course. Anything for me?" "Tomorrow is Wednesday and that means traffic personified, so if you don't mind helping out at Tuolumne, you would be my best friend?" "No problem. Glad to help out. If the higher-ups choose to capture and tag that bear I suggest using a culvert as it is more humane and easily transported." "Will pass it along Mike. Have a good evening. No need to call in the morning unless something comes up." "Thanks, Mike out."

Chapter Five

Mike lay on his back, in his sleeping bag, with his arms cradling his head. The sun was just barely coming up, promising to be another beautiful sunrise. It was already mid June. Where had the time gone, he wondered? As he lay there he thought about how the season had progressed so far and it was a good feeling. Bear sightings were down slightly, compared to the previous year and that was definitely good.

The capturing and killing of bears peaked in 1978 with one hundred and sixty. A plan was set up in 1975 to better manage and handle problem bears in the park. As a direct result of implementing the plan, only twenty-five bears had to be put down in 1992. The bears in Yosemite are black bears. The last grizzly in Yosemite was killed in 1895 and it was estimated to be ten feet tall. "Well, time to get it in gear," said Mike as he threw back the flap and crawled out of the bag. It took just a few seconds to roll and tie it up with a strip of rawhide. Fifteen minutes later, he cranked over the Wrangler's engine and he was on his way.

It was only eight o'clock and the roads were already starting to jam up. Impatient drivers lay on their vehicle's horns as if that action would speed up the process of parking and getting the permits for their stay at Yosemite. The distance from The Valley and Tuolumne was less than an hour and Mike had been on the road for forty-five minutes when he finally inched the jeep into its spot in the parking lot. As he sat in the

33

jeep he looked at the faces of several guests as they quickly walked up to the door to the Tuolumne Center. Most of them had a tight lipped expression and a deep frown on their forehead. *It's going to be a long day,* Mike told himself.

Taking a deep breath to mentally relax, he opened the jeep's door and slid out from behind the wheel. Immediately someone bumped into the door as they walked past. Not a word of apology was said. As Mike walked the short distance to check in at the desk he saw a ranger standing in front of a small group of guests. Several of the guests were holding sheets of paper so he reasoned, they had already checked in, received their permits and were getting a 'Welcome to Yosemite' talk by a female ranger. As Mike passed the group he caught the ranger's eye in passing and each nodded a silent greeting and he heard her southern accent as she talked. Her voice was pleasant to the ear.

Entering the visitor center Mike checked in at the front desk and said he was there to help out for the day. The receptionist's smile lit up his entire face as he said, "Thank you! It has been very busy and I was concerned if HQ would send someone. If you don't mind helping out front with traffic and greeting that would be wonderful." "Will do." As Mike turned to go outside, he heard the raised voice of someone complaining about paying $30 for their vehicle. It didn't take but a few seconds to find the owner of the agitated voice. "Can I help?" Asked Mike as he stood at the side of a middle aged, gray haired man who could easily pass as a lumberjack.

The man turned to face him and the two of them looked at each other. He had a full beard, slightly graying at the temples, bushy eyebrows and steel gray eyes. He wore a black, knitted, rolled at the edges, cap. "If you can explain why it is necessary to charge an exorbitant fee of $30 to drive in the park, then yes, you can help?" asked the man as he crossed his arms across his chest. "The fee is for a seven day pass and is used primarily to maintain the roads during Summer and Winter and maintenance of the park. As the park is open year round entrance fees help us to keep the park in good working order," answered Mike," Also, we are making plans to expand the parking at the visitor centers, lodges and camping areas throughout the park to alleviate some of the congestion. I apologize for any inconvenience, but I assure you no money is wasted in our efforts to see that your experience here at Yosemite is a happy one. I will take note of your concerns and if you will leave your name with the front desk, I will keep you informed with progress as it comes to reality." Mike's relaxed manner and easy way of speaking eased the guests' concerns and the two of them shook hands.

The entire affair had been witnessed by the Center's manager and she walked over and introduced herself. "Mr. Murphy, Barbara Sanders. I didn't mean to eavesdrop, but when I heard a visitor complaining, I came to investigate, but you were already engaged with the guest. You handled the problem quickly and very professionally. I realize the vehicle fee may be a little

35

expensive for some guests, but in all reality, it is necessary if roads are to be maintained throughout the year. In several meetings the problem of parking has come up and we hope to greatly improve conditions over a two year period. This year it has been forecasted, we will again surpass the four million mark in visitor attendance. I understand you were assigned to help out with traffic control and visitor greeting?" "Yes, Ma-am, I saw Ruth out front as I was coming in so I'll give her a hand."Mike opened the front door to go out and a blast warm air hit him in the face. True, it was mid-June and temperatures were warming up quickly after a particularly cold Winter. If the conditions continued the danger of fires would increase dramatically. In 2004 a fire in the Western part of the park burned a little over 3,500 acres and threatened a grove of majestic Sequoia trees.

As Mike approached Ruth he heard part of her 'Welcome to Yosemite Park' greeting. "Approximately 4,000 years ago the park and some of the area around it was inhabited by Ahwaneechee Native Americans. In 1827 trappers found the area and in 1848 gold was discovered. The gold rush brought thousands more people to the area and disputes became an everyday event which helped to spark the Mariposa Indian war which lasted until 1854. Actual tourism of the park began a year later and last year a new record for attendance was set at a little over four million."Ruth's talk continued for a few minutes more and then she asked if there were any questions. One lady asked about taking precautions if a bear was seen. Ruth explained, "Simply, don't move or make a lot of noise. Bears may bluff charge and stop a few yards away then retreat. There has never been a fatality between bears and guests. Throughout the park you will see signs with a red bear on it. These do not mean it is a bear crossing, it is a reminder to slow down when operating your vehicle.

Then a gentleman had a question about hunters and their guns? "Recreational hunting in Yosemite is absolutely forbidden," answered Ruth," The penalties for doing so are quite severe. Any more questions? If not, then please enjoy your stay and don't forget to fill out a guest feedback form, at any visitor center, before leaving to go back home. It is your feedback that helps us to do a better job." Then the group dispersed to find their vehicles and start their vacations. During Ruth's talk Mike had been standing slightly to her left and behind. She turned and asked," How did I do?" "Very good Ruth with just one correction, the Mariposa War ended in 1851. Other than that, it was very informative, especially the part about bear safety." "Thanks Mike, I'll make the correction for next time. I was very nervous the whole time. I'm not all that comfortable standing in front of a group. I feel sort of jammed together. Actually, I prefer to be out in the open. I guess I need to work on my people skills." "Not according to what I heard and saw. You handled yourself smoothly and fielded the questions quickly with good answers."

Then Ruth's cell phone rang and as she took it out of her pants pocket , glanced at it and said, "It's Gladys, excuse me. Yes, Gladys. Yes, he's here. I understand. Thank you." Then Ruth closed the phone and returned it to her pocket. "Gladys asked if I could investigate a couple of bear sightings. One up around Backpackers and another at Miguel Meadow, close to Lake Eleanor."

"Do me a favor Ruth, when you get to Backpackers try and get as accurate a description as possible of the bear, such as scars, male female or anything that would help to positively identify it. There had been earlier reports of bears in that area and we're trying to determine if it's the same one. About that sighting at Miguel Meadow, it could be Big Foot and not a bear." "Big foot here in Yosemite? You're joshing me, right?" "No, seriously. Back in 2004 a guest said they were scared out their wits by something that stood over six feet high and weighed over five hundred pounds." "Mike, really. I think you're pulling my leg." "Well, not exactly," said Mike as he chuckled," It was in all probability a large bear standing upright and at night, one's imagination can play tricks. But there was a probable Big Foot sighting up in that area in 2004, so who knows?"

"Thanks for the heads-up and I'll take it under advisement about that Big Foot sighting. Plus whatever information I gather about Backpackers I'll relay back through Gladys." "Works for me Ruth, have a good one." As Mike watched Ruth walk away to find her vehicle he told himself he thought she had a good sense of humor and even though she said she felt uncomfortable in front of people, her manner said otherwise. She would make a fine ranger ,if she stayed long enough.

For the remainder of the morning and into late afternoon Mike stayed at Tuolumne and stood in front of many small groups of guests as they came out of The Center, after getting their passes and permits. Occasionally a member of The Center's staff would come out and relieve him to take a break or get lunch. As the day progressed so did the temperature and several times, between talking to groups, he took his handkerchief out of his pants pocket, removed his hat and wiped the sweat from his hair and forehead. *I'm definitely going to need that shower tonight.*

Mike had arrived at Tuolumne right at nine AM and it was now five PM. For the last two hours the traffic had been sporadic. At five-thirty a young man came out of the Center and walked over to where he was addressing a group of four people. "Mrs. Sanders said to come out and relieve you for the day and tell you she greatly appreciates your help. She also said to call in and talk to Gladys." "Will do and thank you." Mike stood to the side as the young man started talking and he quickly realized the group was in good hands so he excused himself and went inside The Center. As soon as he opened the Center's door a waft of refrigerated air blew across his face. He just stood there for a few brief seconds, letting the cool breeze wash over him. He wasn't a big fan of all the modern conveniences the world offered, but today could very well be an exception. Mike quickly found a water fountain and as the cold water went down his throat it instantly cooled his whole body. It had to be pushing ninety degrees outside, Mike told himself.

Looking around, he spotted the front desk and walked over. "Any idea how hot it is today?" He asked a young lady. She bent down and looked at a computer screen, then raised her head and answered," Yes, Sir. At the moment it is eight-nine degrees. The forecast is slightly warmer tomorrow with a fifty percent chance of rain showers." "Thank you," said Mike as he turned and walked to the front door where he hesitated slightly before opening it, then went outside.

The air was hot and stuffy with very little wind as he walked to where the jeep was parked. Well, at least there isn't much wind, he reasoned. If the wind was stronger, it could almost be called a Santa Anna like around L.A. That area had already been hit by several fires caused by excessive heat and strong winds. I better check in and see what Gladys called about. "Mike to base?" "Yes, Mike," came a quick reply from Louise. "Gladys has been running around all morning attending meetings, but she asked if you could drop by Sunrise Campground on your way in?" "Sure Louise, it's right on the way. Something wrong?" "Gladys took the call and after she disconnected she just shook her head. Apparently a bear charged a guest, knocked her down and then retreated. The report came in at four-forty-five. This sounds bad Mike, doesn't it?" "Yes, it does. After I check it out I'll call in. It could be around six or so. How late are you staying?" "Till seven as it is my long day." "Thanks. Hopefully it is a false alarm. Mike out."

Chapter Six

Mike was in no hurry to get to Sunrise Campground. According to what Gladys had told him, the bear had actually charged and knocked down a guest. In the entire five years he had been a ranger at the park Mike had never put down a bear, or any other animal. To him all life was precious. The first day back from vacation he had taken his rifle, a Weatherby Mark V out of storage and put it in a locked box in the Wrangler. Mike favored the Weatherby because of its range and stopping power. Fitted with a 6-24x50 Sightron LRMD scope, he could hit anything within 700 yards with ease. In less than fifteen minutes he pulled up to a parking spot at Sunrise and sat for a minute to relax and collect his thoughts. He was not a deeply religious man,but in his heart he wished the report, called in by Mrs. Chandler had been in error.

The late afternoon sun was hot and very little breeze helped to ease his mood as he parked the jeep at a picnic area close to Tenaya Lake. As always, he had his backpack ready to do so it was just a matter of slinging it across his shoulders and start walking. Sunrise Campground was roughly three miles from where he had parked the jeep, a good stretch of the legs.

At the campgrounds there were several groups of people sitting on chairs around campfires."Good afternoon, Mike Murphy, Park Ranger," he said to one group to introduce himself. "I understand a bear charged and knocked down a visitor?" "You understand correctly," said a woman sitting on a stool. "My friends and I was sitting at our table having a late afternoon meal, when this big bear came into our camp, raised up, knocked over the table, scattering our food all over the place, then proceeded to eat it as well as a large bag of apples in our tent." "In the report you said the bear charged and knocked you down?" "I was a little hasty about that and I apologize. After the bear finished with the apples it came to where we were sitting and put its paws on the table, knocking it down. The move scared us and we got out of its way as quickly as possible. After it finished eating it just walked off into the woods as if nothing had happened." Mike thanked the woman and members of her party for the corrected information and excused himself to talk to another group of campers.

They too were sitting at a small portable table eating what looked like home-made hamburgers. "Excuse me," said Mike, as he approached the group. "Mike Murphy, Park Ranger. I understand you had a visit from a bear earlier?" "Quite, Mr. Murphy, "said a man who had a distinct European accent.

"We observed the entire incident. The clumsy cow favored her food over personal safety and stood between the bear and some food they were eating. The bear came out of the forest, there," said the gentleman as he pointed to his left," Proceeded to investigate a tent, then walked or perhaps rambled to their table and finished their dinner. The other members of her party exhibited excellent judgment and safely retreated to their vehicles while she remained, stood in front of their table and yelled at the bear, stepped backwards and tripped over her own feet. After the bear finished, it simply went back into the forest at the same spot it came out of." "Thank you, Mister...?" " Smythe, Reginald Smythe. We are abroad for the Summer and I dare say we are fairly impressed with your park and its ruggedness." "Again, thank you, Mr. Smythe and I hope the remainder of your stay is a complete success."

Mike excused himself and walked over to where Mr. Smythe had said the bear went back into the forest. As he stood before the spot he looked carefully and saw a small opening in the brush. He pulled back the brush to reveal a well worn path on the forest floor. Remembering some research he had done on black bears, Mike recalled they would often use the same game trails year after year walking in the same footsteps. Unfortunately, the area he was looking at was too hard and well packed to reveal any discernible tracks. Upon walking a short distance down the trail Mike came to an area that was covered by loose dirt. As he bent down, he could clearly see a zigzag line of tracks left by a bear. He estimated the tracks to be between four and five inches across. He also noticed a claw was missing on one of the front paws. This piece of information would come in handy when it came time to capture and tag the bear.

According to the tracks it was a single animal and identified by the Franklin boys as female. Armed with this information he called the District office. "Mike to base." "Yes, Mike," answered the voice of Louise, "Did you get a report about the bear at Sunrise Camp?"

"Yes, I did and it was a false alarm." "Thank God! I

was so worried a bear had actually charged a guest and possibly harmed them." "No, the lady who called in evidently forgot how to manage interactions with bears and by her own statement no one was charged or injured. The incident was witnessed by another group and corroborated completely. Please relay the information to Gladys in the morning and thank you for staying over." "No problem Mike. I could not have rested comfortably tonight not knowing if the report was true." "I'm with you, Louise, one hundred percent. I'll check into Valley for the evening and call in tomorrow morning, first thing after breakfast, of course." "Have a good one. Base out."

By the time Mike had checked out the bear sighting at Sunrise and got back on the road it was late afternoon. The air was still hot and stuffy as the day had not given up its heat just yet. The Wrangler did not have AC but being a jeep it was open all around and as he drove down the road the wind felt good. He reached up with one hand and took off his ranger hat and placed it on the passenger seat. His close cut hair helped to dry the small amount of perspiration from his head. Deep inside, he was glad the report of a bear charging a guest had been false. He had the authority to put down a bear, if absolutely necessary to preserve the safety of guests, but he did not relish the idea at all.

From Tanaya Lake to Valley Visitor Center was usually thirty minutes driving time, but this afternoon he was in a hurry to get there and take a hot shower. Even if the day had been sweltering hot, like today, he always favored taking a shower as it helped to relax tense muscles and clear his head before going to bed. In the field, the water of a stream or lake was cool and even cold, but did little to rid his body of stress and tension accumulated during the day. In the military, he had been a Navy seal and had learned to ignore pain and discomfort, but as a civilian he had not had to rely on that training. Also, while he was in the field, he preferred to drive the jeep Wrangler as it had four-wheel capabilities and sometimes he had to go off road to investigate a bear sighting at a campground that was only accessible by backpacking. In the park itself, motorized ATV's were not permitted.

The next morning Mike awoke, stretched and took a deep breath. He had slept soundly all night, which was something he had not done in a while. After a breakfast of hotcakes, scrambled eggs, wheat toast, bacon and steaming hot, black coffee he called in. "Mike to base." "Base to Mike," answered the familiar voice of Louise. "I trust you had a good evening and slept well?" "Yes, best I've slept in some time, thank you. Anything for me today?" "No, nothing came in. Oh, almost forgot, Mr. Summers is back from his leave of absence. He said everything is fine. He apologized for the secretiveness and said his wife did have cancer, but with the chemo treatments it has gone into remission. Other than that Mike, I guess you are free to do your normal routine." "Thanks, glad to hear about Mr. Summers. I have been wanting to do some backpacking along Delaney Creek, just to see how things look. It is about mid-season and there aren't any campsites in that area, but you never know." "Okay, will call on your cell if anything turns up that needs your attention." "Thanks Louise, Mike out."

It had been some time since he had been backpacking and he looked forward to being away from the office, even if it was only temporary. He loved his job as a park ranger and the outdoors, but sometimes dealing with rude people pushed the envelope of his patience. As he looked over the items spread out over the bed in his room, he mentally ran over a list of what to take and he remembered what one of the Franklin boys had said, FISHFRINN. He chuckled and shook his head, the acronym was correct and included everything that might be needed while backpacking. Yesterday morning, he had followed up on his promise of writing a letter of recognition and commendation for the boys.

As he slung the pack onto his shoulders and shook it back and forth to settle it, he estimated it to weigh between fifteen and twenty pounds. He was in great shape, both physically and mentally to begin the hike, so with a hand wave at the desk clerk on his way out, he was on his way. Somehow the air smelled especially clean that morning as he set an easy stride that was both comfortable and easy to maintain. His planned route would be from The Center, to Delaney Creek to Glen Aulin. From Tuolumne Center to Delaney Creek was less than two miles, as the crow flies. From the Center to Glen Aulin was about five and a half miles, most of which was over rugged terrain. Once Mike established an easy pace it was simply a matter of putting one foot in front of another. The air was fresh and did not smell of exhaust fumes from vehicles.

Once he crossed the bridge, just past the Tuolumne Center, he made a right turn and briefly stopped for a breather. From here on the hike would be over rocky ground, slabs of granite and small ponds until he reached the southern end of the trail at Delaney Creek. Along the route he saw several Golden Mantled ground squirrels and even a mule deer. The pace Mike had set earlier paid off and in quick time he arrived at Glen Aulin. The view was magnificent! As he looked around, he saw, Mt. Dana, Mt. Gibbs and Kuna Crest. The meadow itself was wide and open surrounded by tall evergreen trees with the Conness Creek meandering through it. Taking a pair of field glasses from his pack, Mike scanned over the area and did not see anything out of the ordinary. There were a few backpackers and as he observed them, they looked like they were experienced hikers. He had started out early in the morning and now it was mid-afternoon, so the only thing left to do was find a suitable spot to camp for the evening. It had been a good day to hike and even being in excellent physical shape, his body told him he needed to get out more. In no time he set up his sleeping bag and started a small fire. The fire wasn't needed as it was relatively warm, but it helped, psychologically to sit beside its warmth and unwind from the day's activities. He slept soundly and woke up the next morning and the air smelled strongly of decaying flesh. Sitting up, Mike turned into the wind, it was coming from directly behind him in the trees.

Chapter Seven

Something was definitely not right. Scrambling out of his sleeping bag, Mike reached down to his backpack, got out his field glasses and did a quick scan at the tree line and the surrounding area. The search revealed nothing out of place. *Well, nothing to do but investigate,* he told himself. Forgetting about his morning routine, brushing his teeth and making coffee, Mike quickly packed everything up and put it away in the backpack. Once again, he shrugged his shoulders to settle in the pack and then he set out to investigate the smell of carrion that was overpowering everything else that morning.

As the ground was mostly rock and granite there wasn't much open ground to identify anything and help solve the mystery. It only took a few minutes of fast walking to arrive at the tree line surrounding the meadow. Precaution was the key element here as dead animals were not the norm in the park. It could even be a dead human. The smell was even stronger and Mike knew he was very close to finding out what the cause of it was. Proceeding carefully into the woods, Mike looked around at the vegetation and earth, nothing seemed amiss until he came to a small clearing. In the clearing was a tent torn to shreds and the carcass of a black bear.

The smell of rotting flesh was overpowering and he had to wrap a bandana around his head and over his mouth so he could breathe. Mike's first impression of the scene in front of him was the bear destroyed the tent while searching for food, but what or who had killed the bear? Kneeling over the remains of the bear, it was impossible to determine how the bear died. Scavengers had been at the carcass and only the fur, bones and a few pieces of rotting flesh, were left.

The clearing itself was about thirty feet in diameter and the ground was mostly soft dirt and a few small rocks. As Mike looked closer at the ground, he saw many tracks of what resembled those of ATV's and dirt bikes which were not permitted in the park. Retreating out of the woods to get some fresh air, Mike called Gladys on his cell phone. She answered on the first ring. "Good morning Mike. Everything okay? Why the cell?" "No, things are not quite okay," answered Mike," I'm up here at Glen Aulin. I backpacked in from Delaney Creek and found the carcass of a bear. Apparently it has been dead a few days. No indication how it died as the only thing left is a few bones and scraps of flesh. The remains of a tent, torn to shreds, probably by the bear was at the site. One thing, however, has anyone checked in, that you know of, that had four wheelers or dirt bikes on trailers?" "Four wheelers as in ATV's?" "Yes, exactly, or better yet check and see if any guests have permits to backpack up around Glen Aulin? I saw several on my way in." "Will do Mike and I'll get back to you. Should I let the boss know?" "Yes."

Mike did not relish the thought of going back to where the carcass was but it had to be done. Folding up his cell phone, Mike once again wrapped his bandana to cover his mouth and nose, but first he spilled a small amount of water, from his canteen onto the cloth as a filter against the powerful odor. In the short time since he had been at the site a strong breeze from the south had sprung up carrying the odor back into the woods. Mike rationalized, this was probably why he had not noticed it earlier. With the wind blowing in the opposite direction Mike was able to walk around the site freely in an attempt to gather as much information as possible to solve the mystery.

There were a few boot prints, but they were so old no discernible markings could be gathered other than they were of heavy duty material. About a half hour after he had called Gladys, his cell phone rang again. "Mike, the boss said to collect as much evidence as you can, take a sample of the bear to help in finding out how it died and then bury the carcass if you can. Also, if the tent has any identifying marks write them down, to aid in the investigation." "Will do Gladys. I'll call in when I get back to Tuolumne, after getting things squared away here."

In keeping with the scout motto of 'Be Prepared' Mike carried a small collapsible shovel, strapped to the back of his pack with a bungee cord. After carefully taking a few samples of fur and flesh from the bear carcass, Mike double wrapped them in plastic baggies and stowed them away in his pack. Then came the task of burying the remains of the bear to avoid possible poisoning any animals. As the ground was mostly dirt it didn't take long to dig a suitable hole to bury the carcass and the tent. The tent was a standard two person, light green, canvass rig with a front zipper and no markings to distinguish it from thousands of other tents. An hour later Mike once again packed up his gear and after looking around the area to make sure the burial site was well covered and indiscernible to the naked eye, he started the trek back to Tuolumne.

About half way back on the return trip, Mike encountered a group of four backpacker's apparently on their way up to Glen Aulin. "Good morning," said Mike. "You folks are out early. Planning on a day at Glen Aulin?" "Actually, we are going a bit further northwest to Waterwheel Falls. We are part of a naturalist group doing a term paper for college. You're a park ranger?" "Yes. Mike Murphy, I was just up a little north of Glen Aulin myself this morning. A good day for a hike." Everyone in the group and Mike exchanged handshakes and a man, apparently the leader of the group asked," Anything we should watch out for this morning? Animals, weather?" "None that I am aware of but please observe all precautions around animals, especially bears." "One item, before we left to begin our trip we took the precaution of getting Hanta virus inoculations.

A few years ago, there were incidents here in the park. Is that all cleared up now?" "Yes, completely and no cause for alarm," answered Mike. "We should finish up with taking photographs and gathering data early this afternoon, but if not we will stay the night at Glen Aulin and make our way back in the morning." "Sounds like a good plan," agreed Mike. "If you run into trouble of any sort use the park number 209-372-0200 to call for assistance." "Thank you Mike for the heads-up." "You're welcome and please have a good day."

By the time Mike had hiked back to Tuolumne Center Gladys had followed up on checking for guests with ATV's or dirt bikes and as soon as he got to the Wrangler he checked in. "Yes, Mike so glad you called. I checked and four male guests checked in through the Tioga Pass entrance two weeks ago. They said they were on their way to Las Vegas for a motocross event and decided to stay overnight to rest up before continuing on. The strange thing is they never actually stayed at the Tuolumne Meadows campground." "Thanks Gladys. Please relay all information to the boss. I'll drive on in to Valley and call in the morning." "Have a good evening." That night, after getting a meal and taking a hot shower, Mike sat on the open veranda of his room at Valley.

The air was still slightly warm from the day, but a good breeze was blowing. There weren't any typical early evening noises such as frogs or crickets to disturb the mood, so Mike sat back in his comfortable chair and closed his eyes. The sound of someone knocking on his door woke him up. He quickly glanced at his watch and it read seven AM, he had slept completely through the night. As he approached the door a voice on the other side asked, "Room service. Do you need clean towels Mr. Mike?" Opening the door, he saw the familiar face of Rosa. Her arms were full of white towels. "Good morning Rosa. Yes. I got in late last night and was really tired. Just a large bath towel and wash cloth will do. Thank you."

He must have been really tired to sleep through the night sitting in a chair. The only thing that made sense was that he was not used to backpacking. He was in good shape and the pack had not been that heavy. As he stood at the bathroom sink, brushing his teeth, he looked at himself in the mirror. Was he getting old? His hair was still dark brown with no graying at the temples. A few wrinkles around the eyes, but that could be explained as he did not always wear his sunglasses outdoors and he would squint because of the brightness. After brushing his hair, he took a deep breath and shook his head. Perhaps getting old, just a little. Downstairs he found a hearty breakfast to start the day. It was now eight o'clock and time to check in.

"Mike to base." "Good morning Mike," answered Louise. "You're at The Valley, correct?" "Yes. Got in late. What's up?" "It's been a madhouse around here. Traffic jams, angry guests complaining about park fees and four reports of bear sightings." "Did you call in off duty rangers to help out?" "Not yet, was waiting for Mr. Summers to get in." "Look at the roster of off duty rangers and call in two who have the lowest seniority. I don't think Mr. Summers would have a problem with that, but in case he does I'll come in for a face to face. Where were the bear sightings?" "Up at Backpackers. Within a three hour period four bears, without cubs, visited tents scrounging for food and broke a car window to get at some fruit that was left in there by mistake. One other thing Mike, the bear that broke the car window evidently injured itself. There were a few drops of blood on the ground." "Okay. Thanks for hanging in there Louise. How's the baby?" "Doing just fine. We went and had a sonogram done and it's going to be a boy." "Congratulations. I will head on up to Backpackers and call in after I investigate and gather information." "Good luck and have a good one. Base out."

As Mike drove up to Backpackers he thought about what Louise had told him. Four bears in a three hour period? That was highly unusual. Bear sightings were just about an everyday occurrence, especially now as they were making every effort to get ready for hibernation. Over the years bears in the park had become accustomed to human food as it contained more calories than berries and nuts. Bears will also eat insect larvae, ants and termites, they find in rotten logs. An adult bear will sometimes consume close to 20,000 calories a day in preparing for hibernation, especially if it is late in the year. One curious fact about hibernating bears; they do not defecate or urinate the entire time of hibernation.

Hibernating bears in the park usually choose, tree branches, rotting logs and holes formed by rocks jumbled together. During this time two to three cubs are born that weigh about a pound and a half at birth. If a bear did not put on enough weight to sustain herself and her cubs through hibernation, she would terminate the pregnancy to preserve her own health. During the forty-five minute drive to Backpackers Mike thought about Louise and her report about one of the bears injuring itself getting to the fruit in the car. The cardinal rule in hunting is that you do not pursue an injured animal until a reasonable amount of time has passed allowing the animal to die. An injured animal is very dangerous. Mike's thoughts went to the Weatherby stowed away in its locker and he prayed he would not have to use it. Almost exactly forty-five minutes later, Mike pulled into the parking area at Backpackers. Several small groups were standing around, talking loudly and waving their arms. Straightening his hat and putting on his sunglasses, Mike looked at himself in the Wrangler's rear-view mirror, took a deep breath and exited the jeep.

Chapter Eight

This was one part of being a park ranger Mike did not enjoy. Anytime a bear was injured, regardless of the cause, it came with the possibility he would have to put down the bear. Well, no getting around the issue, it had to be addressed and resolved. As he approached the campers, a few recognized his uniform and walked in his direction. Mike quickly read their mannerisms and decided they were not angry, just a little shaken up. "Good morning, Mike Murphy, park ranger. I understand you had a visitor and a little excitement this morning?"

"Yes, you could say that," said one of the men. "Samuel Goldman, adjuster for Midlothian insurance. My wife and I are celebrating our twenty-fifth wedding anniversary and have never been to Yosemite. We both enjoy camping so decided to rough it for a few days. Our visitor, or visitors, arrived right after five-thirty and proceeded to check our tent for anything edible and finding none went on to the next tent where it found some chips or something in a bag, anyway. There were two of them, adults, fairly good sized without any cubs. Finding nothing more worth eating they returned to the woods behind the tents. A short time later, maybe twenty-minutes, two more visited. Except these two came from over there," explained Mr. Goldman as he pointed across the meadow. "Did these two also raid the tents?" Asked Mike. "No, well one of them casually walked around the camp, sniffing the wind and the other one broke a car window to get at something left in the back seat. I think the animal may have injured itself because there were some drops of blood on the ground by the vehicle. After it ate whatever was in the bag, it sort of limped off into the woods over there behind the tents."

After chatting with a few more guests at the campsite, Mike gathered enough information to corroborate what Mr. Goldman had told him and he did not like it; he was dealing with an injured animal. From where he was standing Mike could see the vehicle that had been broken into. It was a Ford Bronco and the rear window had been completely smashed in. As he advanced toward the SUV, Mike carefully looked at the ground to see if any prints had been left behind. Luck was with him and the soft earth was full of fresh prints. One set was slightly larger and had a missing claw on a front paw. It was the same female identified by the Franklin boys and from what Mike could see was the one that injured itself.

With a heaviness in his chest Mike went to the Wrangler and unlocked the gun case holding the Weatherby. Slinging the weapon across his shoulders and putting a handful of shells in his pants pocket, he proceeded to cautiously walk down a narrow trail the guests had said the injured bear had gone down. His senses on full alert, Mike slowly placed one foot in front of the other looking in all directions simultaneously. The ground here was also soft dirt and the tracks were clearly visible. Looking at the tracks Mike could see a few scattered drops of blood. Mr. Goldman had said the bear limped so that told Mike the injured part was a leg or paw. By the small amount of blood the wound probably was not that bad, but any wounded animal is dangerous. Mike reached to his shoulder and grasped the rifle, then carried it across his body with both hands. The forest was strangely silent as he continued further down the narrow trail into the woods.

A bird suddenly took flight and he unconsciously brought the rifle to bear directly out in front of him. His heart was pounding! It was a false alarm. It took a few minutes for him to settle down his jangled nerves. This was dangerous business tracking an injured animal. After about fifteen minutes of slow and meticulous following the bear's tracks, they led him to a broad patch of hard ground, littered with rocks and boulders. Actually, Mike was relieved the trail could not be followed any further and returned to the campsite, put the rifle back in its case and locked it.

Sitting on the jeep's side step, Mike removed his sunglasses and briefly closed his eyes. Hearing the approach of footsteps on gravel, he opened his eyes to see another of the campers who had described the bears. "Yes?" He asked. "Mr. Murphy, I don't mean to intrude, but did you find the bears?" "No. I followed the trail of the injured one, but lost it among the rocks and boulders." "I was concerned you might have to shoot it. I am a tracker by trade and know the dangers a wounded animal can bring. "Thomas Mitchell," said the man as he extended his hand. Mike didn't say anything as he looked at the man in front of him; lightweight tan jacket, sturdy brown corduroy pants, heavy-duty leather, hiking boots and a tanned almost leathery face under a floppy camouflage hat. He had a distinct accent "I'm sorry, asked Mike," What was it you said?" "Thomas Mitchell, tracker, out of Brisbane."

"Yes, thank you. Apologies. I never like the idea of having to put down an animal. I lost the trail in some rocks. You say you're a tracker by trade?" "Yes, Sir. Tracked everything from crocodiles to gorillas. I do not use dogs as they might get killed or injured. If possible I prefer to trap and relocate in place of killing." "Mr. Mitchell, speaking for the park, would you like to help locate, trap and tag the bear I was tracking earlier. Whatever you require for a fee, within reason, is acceptable." "Certainly. If we will be tagging and releasing the bear. I will waive any fee." Mike felt a deep sense of relief flood over his body. Finally, a decent human being among the madness of the world. "I'll call the office and have them airlift a culvert trap. Shouldn't be more than an hour at the most." Ten minutes later Gladys called back over the jeep radio.

"Yes, Gladys?" "Sorry Mike but a chopper won't be available until first light in the morning. The boss approved the use of both the chopper and the culvert trap. You say you enlisted the help of a professional tracker?" "Yes. A Mr. Mitchell and he said to waive his normal fee." "Thanks Mike, I'll relay that bit of information to Mr. Summers when he comes out of a meeting." "Thanks Gladys. We will make do here and call at first light as to where to set the culvert down.

Mike out."

Mr. Mitchell was standing beside Mike as he was talking to Gladys and when Mike finished, he said," Well, Mr. Murphy it looks like we are on our own until morning. I brought some extra gear in case of a lengthy stay so what do you say we find a suitable spot and set up camp for the evening?" An hour later they were sitting around a small fire and enjoying a meal of pemmican, beef jerky and chicken MRE's. (Meals Ready To Eat) The pemmican and MRE's were provided by Mr. Mitchell and the beef jerky by Mike. With full stomachs they crawled into their sleeping bags and fifteen minutes were soundly asleep. In a few hours they were rudely awakened by the distinctive sound of a helicopter beating the air with its rotors. It was what is referred to as false dawn and the morning sky was just barely starting to show some color. Mike glanced at his wrist-watch, pushed a button, and in its light green florescence could tell it was five AM. *Well, Gladys did say at first light* , he told himself. Rolling out of his sleeping bag Mike glanced over towards Mr. Mitchell's bed, it was empty.

Just as Mike finished rolling up his sleeping bag, Mr. Mitchell walked up and said, "Goday' mate. Got up early and made my way to the 'crik to freshen up for the day and call me Tom." "Morning Tom. The culvert is already here. You ready to go to work?" "Born ready. Let's get to it." The jeep's radio crackled to life. "Chopper to Murphy. Where do you want this thing?" Quickly Mike ran over and grabbed the microphone."Murphy here.

There's a small clearing about a half mile due north of the camp. Drop it in there if you can, or as close to there as possible." "Roger."

As Mike and Tom watched, the chopper banked to the right and with the culvert trap slung underneath, was quickly out of sight. They were alone as everyone else had left late, the same afternoon as Mike had arrived at the campsite. "If it's okay, I'll lead to where I lost the trail and then you take over," suggested Mike. "Tally ho, as the Brits say."

They made quick time to where the chopper had left the culvert trap and immediately began to camouflage it to look like the surrounding area. Mike did not open the gate as it was remotely controlled from a handheld device. After they had found enough branches and brush to hide the trap, they explored around the area and found a hidden vantage point about thirty yards away from which they could observe the trap door.

"How do you want to manage this?" asked Tom " "It's a good area and coming in I spotted several promising tracks going to the campsite but none coming back. It seems the bears circle the camp when tourists are there in search for food and then retreat. Strange behavior for bears. We could pack a few supplies for a day, maybe two and scout around before baiting the trap. My time is yours." "Sounds like a good plan. But first, let's go back to the camp and I'll call in to the office and find out what bears are in the area. If we spot any, we can match them against their GPS tags. If no tag, there's a high probability it will be the bear we are after as she has not yet been tagged. Also, the bear we want is probably slightly injured, front paw." "Sounds like a good plan," agreed Tom.

After exploring around the area, for the better part of a day, they did not see a single bear, but according to their tags, they were within a five mile radius of the camp. They talked it over and decided to go ahead, bait the trap and wait. Mike had brought along some apples he had been saving for a snack and a small plastic bag filled with scraps from the campsite's refuse barrels. Leaving Tom with the remote, Mike took the bait and when Tom opened the door, he placed it at the far end of the trap. Now the only thing to do was hope the right bear couldn't resist the lure and enter the trap. It didn't take long and right before sundown Tom reached over and nudged Mike, who was looking in the opposite direction. "Tally ho, mate, we have a visitor," he whispered. Mike turned and raised his field glasses to where Tom was looking. "That's her," Mike confirmed as he spotted a slight limp in her gait. "It's your show," whispered Mike as he handed the remote to Tom.

Out of the corner of one eye, Mike looked at Tom, grasping the remote in one hand and with the other holding his binoculars up to his eyes. Mike's mouth was taking in short breaths. He watched through his own field glasses as the bear cautiously sniff the air, walk a few steps and again test the air. *She is very careful, this one,* Mike said to himself. *Come on girl, just a little bit more. She's in the trap!*

The next morning a team of veterinarians came up to

the camp and Mike took them to the culvert where the bear had spent the night, safely inside. After she was shot with a tranquilizer dart, they opened the door and applied a thick bandage, to her right front paw, loaded with antibiotics to guard against infection. The vet also attached a GPS ear tag. As Mike watched the lady apply the bandage he asked if it would interfere with her ability to get around? "Not actually, if it doesn't come off by itself in a day, possibly two, she will get tired of it and tear it off." "How about we give her the name Molly?" Suggested Mike. "Molly it is," said a vet as she clicked the tag into place. A half hour later, from a safe observation place, Mike, Tom and the lady vet watched as Molly slowly began to stir and come out from the effects of the tranquilizer dart. A few minutes later she rolled to her feet and slowly walked into the thick underbrush.

"You have a good heart, mate," said Tom as he extended his hand. "That's 'wat it's all about. Any bloke who takes pleasure with loading his den wall with trophies needs to 'ave his head examined." "I couldn't agree with you more," said Mike as they shook hands, then he asked, "So, you have any plans? Family?" "I do. Long overdue for a vacation and 'aven't been home in over two years. Just me, no family to speak of. Sheilas like a man that stays close to home and that sort of life's not for me. As you Yank's say, have a good one." "That I will. You need a lift anywhere?" "No thanks, mate. I still have a few MRE's in my pack and two days left on my vacation so might as well put them to use." Mike watched as Tom slung his backpack across his shoulders and shake it a little to settle it in and then with an easy stride, walked off into the woods.

Chapter Nine

Morning came and Mike was sitting on the veranda of his room. It was Friday. The sun was barely peeking above the horizon, sending shafts of light through the clouds. The sky was ablaze with color. *It was times like these you are glad you're alive*, he told himself. He had already been downstairs for breakfast and it was promising to be a wonderful day. Glancing at his watch he read the time; six-thirty AM. "Well, better call in and see what the office has for me today," said Mike to no one in particular. Before he closed the door of his room behind him, Mike made a mental check of things he might need for the day and satisfied he had everything, closed the door.

Downstairs he waved at the desk clerk and said, "Good morning. I'll be back tonight and if you can have Marie leave some extra towels that would be excellent. Alanah will be checking in late this afternoon for a few days." "She is supposed to graduate this year isn't she?" "Yes, final semester." "I'll tell housekeeping to leave extra towels. Any messages you want to leave for her?" asked Marie. "No, thanks anyway. If I'm going to be later than usual, I'll call and let her know."

"Mike to base." "Good morning Mike," answered Louise. "Getting an early start are we?" "Yes, I'm a work-a-holic, remember? Anything for me?" "Just one item. There was a note left by Gladys about someone hearing gunfire late yesterday afternoon. She was just getting ready to go home and the phone rang. She said

65

the caller was a woman who was vacationing with some friends and were hiking up around Smedberg Lake." "Did she say if it sounded like a handgun or rifle" "She was positive it was a handgun, but she also said there were two booms, like a shotgun. She owns a handgun and knows the sound." "Thanks for the information. Can you check to see if any rangers were in that area?" "Wait one." A few moments later Louise answered, "Good thinking Mike. Yes, rangers Donaldson and Mackenzie responded to a call about a bear sighting and had to fire both blanks and rubber slugs to scare it away." "Thanks Louise. Mike out."

After hanging up the microphone on its hook, Mike sat in the Wrangler's passenger seat and looked at the traffic already starting to gather in the parking lot. July and August both had been extremely busy and only a few thousand guests remained to break the previous record of 4.1 million. There were still four months left in the year.

Alanah had just a few weeks left before graduation and was really looking forward to joining the staff at the park. Earlier they had talked it over and she was considering both a ranger and park PR position. She was coming this weekend to finalize her decision. He was deep in thought when the radio crackled to life, "Base to Mike." "What's up?" he answered. "A report just came in about a bear sighting at Cathedral Beach. Can you check it out?" "No problem. On my way."

Cathedral Beach was less than five miles from where he was so in a few minutes he was getting out of the jeep and walking toward a man and woman sitting at a picnic table. There wasn't anyone else around so he guessed she was the one who had called in. "Good morning, Mike Murphy, park ranger. You called in a bear sighting?" "Yes. My husband and I were just getting up and found this huge bear trying to open our food cooler. We put a lock on it last night and it was a good thing. The bear couldn't open it so just banged it around a little, then walked off in that direction," said the lady as she pointed towards the woods."I don't know if it was a male or female. We were told during our briefing when we got the camping permit to report all bear sightings." "Yes, you did right and thank you. It helps us to keep track of where the bears are at any given time." "You can do that?" She asked. "Yes Ma-am. The bears have a GPS tag and we track them by satellite." "Amazing technology." "Yes Ma-am. If I could ask you to fill out a guest form at a Visitor Center when you are ready to go home, we would greatly appreciate it?" "We certainly will Mr. Murphy. We come to the park every year and haven't missed a trip in over fifteen years." "Excellent! I am sure you have seen many changes the park has undergone, through the years. It is your valuable input that helps us to make sure your next visit will be better than the last one. Is there anything that impresses you most about the changes that have been made or you would like to be made?" "The only thing that comes to mind right away is making the campsites a little less wild. Maybe a few more showers would be very nice." "Yes Ma-am. Please add that to your list of suggestions and leave it at a Visitor Center and have a good day."

He was sure the bear was long gone out of the area, but to be safe Mike decided to walk a little in the direction the lady had pointed. There was actually a small path and from what he could see, the bear had walked a short distance up the trail and then turn off into the thick brush. As Mike turned around to look behind him towards the campgrounds, the bear suddenly rushed out of the bushes onto the trail and bluff charged toward him. The bear's action startled him, but he remembered his training to raise his arms and start yelling. The bear continued to run a short distance until it was less than ten feet away, then it suddenly stopped, clacked its jaws, blew noisily several times then retreated back down the trail until it was out of sight. Mike took a deep breath and slowly let it out. *That was close,* he told himself.

Bears had bluff charged before, but not quite like this one. Keeping a wary eye open Mike walked back to the campsite and checked in. "Yes, Mike go ahead," said Louise. "I'm here at Cathedral Beach. Everything is normal. Just a single sighting, nothing damaged, injured or broken. Will continue on my rounds and be back around six. Mike out." "Oh, wait! You remember that group of guests that came in through the Tioga Pass entrance but didn't check into the Tuolumne Visitor Center?" "Yes, that was a few months ago." "Correct. Mr. Summers filed a report with CHP naming them as possible suspects. Well, it seems the law caught up with them! Apparently they were on their way back from Las Vegas and stopped for a meal in Bridgeport, just outside the park. The local police saw a trailer with dirt bikes and two small ATV's. The trailer's tags were expired and when a search was conducted, their names came up. Their vehicle and all their off road gear were confiscated and right now they are in jail." "That's the best news I have heard in a long time! That made my day. Thank you Louise!" "You're welcome Mike. You say you're going to be in around six?" "Yes, Alanah is coming for the weekend and will be in later this afternoon" "Sounds great. Base out."

The Wrangler was getting low on gas so he drove to Crane Flat, which was about eight miles away and gassed up. While standing at the gas pump Mike noticed a young couple sitting beside their RV at a small folding table. After he hung up the handle, Mike washed his hands using a small amount of water from a bottle he always carried and a couple of sheets of paper towel. Then he walked over to the couple, introduced himself and asked, "How has your vacation been so far? Everything meet your expectations?" "Yes," said the young man. "We're from Fresno and this is our first time. Confirmed city slicker's. My wife and I are just starting a two-week vacation and will spend a few days here then travel on to San Diego. She is fairly impressed with the facilities considering it is outdoors and everything." "Good to hear," said Mike, "If you would, please fill out a guest form at any Visitor Center when you leave. It helps us to do a better job and keep the park running smoothly." "Can do, Mr. Murphy."

The remainder of the round was uneventful and at six PM he pulled into the reserved parking spot at Valley

Center and turned off the ignition. Sitting in the driver's seat, Mike sat for a few seconds to mentally unwind from the day's activities and then he reached over to the handle and opened the door. It was his weekend to be off and what better way than to have Alanah here to help celebrate?

His pace quickened as he walked across the parking lot and opened the door of the Center. Mike waved at the desk clerk as he passed and when the clerk looked up and recognized him said, "Evening Mike. You have a guest. She checked in at three-thirty. I gave her a pass key. Have a good evening." Taking the stairs two at a time Mike ran and opened the door. Alanah was sitting out on the veranda and ran to greet him. They hugged and as soon as she felt the perspiration that had soaked through his shirt declared, "You need a bath." "Yes, Ma-am. Will take care of that right away. You want to have dinner up here or down stairs?" "Up here if that would be okay? The sun will be going down in a little while and watching it from the veranda would be wonderful. I'll call down and see what they have. Any suggestions?" "Steak is a little heavy...?" "Fish it is. Grab your shower and I'll lay out some clothes for you." "Now I know why I married you. You can read minds," said Mike as he chuckled. "Not exactly true, but we have this connection, it's called love. Get your shower." "Yes, Ma-am."

Mike and Alanah had been married almost two years. They had met while Mike was attending a forestry conservation seminar at Berkley. She was already enrolled and on her way to earning a Masters in Forestry

Management. Their engagement lasted a year and they finally tied the knot. At the time Mike was enjoying his first year as a park ranger and it was during that year he decided to get involved in park security, search and rescue. Mr. Summers had talked to him several times and said he had a natural talent for observation, deduction and reasoning, all excellent elements of security work; plus search and rescue would give him hands-on experience as a park ranger.

A half hour later, Mike and Alanah were sitting out on the veranda, eating their dinner of baked salmon cakes, broccoli with cheese sauce, wheat rolls, house salad, white wine and a slice of apple pie. "Mike, would you be upset if I didn't come on board as a park ranger?" Asked Alanah as she pushed away her empty plate. "Of course not Sweetheart. That's your call. But what about your degree?" "Oh, I didn't mean to not be involved in forestry management. Not that at all. What I meant, was doing PR work here in the park." "Sure. There is that and you would be very good at it. You're a much better people person than I am. You want to set up a meeting with Mr. Summers to work out the details?" "Yes, can we do that? I can stay an extra day or two. At this point attendance is a mere formality. I've already taken my finals with just one remaining and that isn't until next week." "I'll set it up with Ryan Monday morning."

The sunset that evening was spectacular with all colors of the light spectrum on display. Alanah moved her chair a little closer to Mike's and laid her head on his shoulder as they sat and watched the sun go down below the horizon. It was a full moon and in its light familiar shapes changed to objects shaded in gray. The day had not yet given up its warmth and the two of them sat on the veranda long into the evening, just enjoying each other's company. Finally, somewhere around midnight they turned in and slept through the night.

Chapter Ten

"Good morning sleepy head," said Mike as he sat the breakfast tray down on the bedside table. "Rise and shine." "Morning already?" Asked Alanah, as she raised up in bed, yawned and then stretched her arms over her head "I was having such a nice dream. We were camping out and it started to snow." "That's not too far off from reality. Usually by mid November Tioga Pass entrance is closed due to snow. Camping out in the snow? I like the snow Sweetheart but when it's forty degrees and the wind is blowing thirty miles an hour you can't put on enough layers to stay warm." "I know, but doesn't it sound romantic, just a little?" "Yes, it does, actually. Just never thought about it quite like that. Glad you're here to keep me in touch with things. Breakfast is getting cold. Let's eat." An hour later they were downstairs standing in the lobby and looking outside through the large windows. It was barely nine AM and the traffic was already starting to build up in the parking lot.

"You have to deal with this every day?" Asked Alanah. "If needed, yes, but my primary job is park security, search and rescue. Other rangers usually handle traffic control and I help out if needed." "So if I chose to go into public relations instead of a ranger like you, any idea what I would be looking at?" "Let's sit, this may take a little time to explain," suggested Mike. "You want something to drink, coffee, tea, soft drink, something stronger?" "Coffee would be fine, decaf with a little creamer, no sugar." "Coming right up, find us a seat."

As the two of them sat in the lobby drinking coffee, Mike explained what little he knew of public relations for the park. "PR, as far as I know includes, heavy media coverage in the event of an incident between animals, primarily bears and guests. There are also film crews from time to time making videos and movies, interactions between international delegates and various park functions. What all that means is you would be involved with people, business meetings and basically anything that has to do with the park and how it is represented to the public. Translated, a lot of hard work. You still want the job?" "Yes." "Great! I was hoping you would say that. I'll set up a meeting with Mr. Summers, first thing Monday morning. The day is just beginning. What do you want to do?" "I rented a car. Could we just drive around so I can get a feel, both visual and physical of the park?" "Sure. We can go by the District Office. I don't know if Gladys will be there, but Louise, the dispatcher will be, I am sure." "No, just you and I would be fine." "Okay. I'll pick up a snack from the kitchen to take along."

For the rest of the day Mike drove the rental car from the Valley Center to, Crane Flat, Tuolumne Meadows Center, the Tioga Road entrance, then back to the Big Oak Flat entrance. After Big Oak Flat, they stopped at Hodgdon Meadow campgrounds and ate the snack Mike had bought before starting out. Sitting at a picnic table they sat across from each other, Mike looked at Alanah and asked," First thoughts?" "I never realized it was so beautiful. I know what forests, rocks and streams look like but put together like this is breathtaking, almost like a miracle." " I never thought of it exactly like that, but yes, I do have to agree with you," said Mike. "We still have a few hours of daylight left. Any ideas?" "None that I can think of. It has been a wonderful day, thank you. I'm going to like my new home." That evening Mike put in a wake-up call at the front desk, for seven AM to give them plenty of time to get up, dressed, have breakfast and go to worship services at 9: 15.

The Yosemite Chapel was originally built-in 1879 on Four Mile Trail and later moved in 1901 to its present site close to Yosemite Lodge. A highlight of its history was a special memorial service held for President Grant. The organist for the occasion was Sir Arthur Sullivan, known for the Gilbert and Sullivan operas.

Monday morning, Mike called and asked if Mr. Summers was in, Gladys said he was but had meetings until ten AM. He then asked if she could set up a meeting between Alanah, himself and Mr. Summers sometime around eleven, before lunch anyway and call back to confirm? She said, no problem. At the office they sat patiently waiting for Mr. Summers to get out of the ten o'clock meeting. Finally, at ten-thirty the board room door opened and Ryan came out. As soon as he saw them, he walked over and extended his hand."Thanks for waiting. You want something to drink? Coffee? Tea?" " We just had breakfast. Thanks. Alanah has decided to apply for the Public Relations position." "Excellent, come on in and we'll talk," suggested Mr. Summers. A half hour later they all shook hands and

Ryan said, "Welcome to the team, Alanah. Glad to have you aboard."

After the meeting with Mr. Summers, Mike said, "Let's have lunch to celebrate. My treat!" "Well, thank you kind Sir. That is mighty magnanimous of you," said Alanah, going along with the spirit of the moment. "Do we need reservations or is it come as you are?" "Oh, I think they can find a nice quiet, out of the way, booth for us. I know the maître d'."

"Seriously, "said Mike, as they sat eating lunch, "It will be hard work until you get used to everything. It's a brand new ballgame and probably different from anything you've experienced before. We have a good, tight-knit crew, but the hard work would be from interacting directly with the public, like a liaison. Most of the time it is simply routine, but Summer months are the most stressful. Even being here five plus years, some days it gets to me. The work itself is enjoyable, I am outdoors, but my people skills are sometimes lacking." "We are a team and together there is nothing we can't handle," said Alanah confidently. "Then here's to us," said Mike as he raised his glass of water in a toast. She raised hers and their glasses clinked together.

All too soon the day finally wound down and after eating dinner, they went upstairs and retired for the evening. The next morning, Alanah left to go back to Berkley and take the last final. Taking the last final was actually just a formality as her GPA was already high enough to graduate Magna Cum Laude.

The rest of the week passed uneventfull and instead of

using the Wrangler's radio to call in Monday morning Mike used the phone at the lobby front desk. "Good morning Gladys. What do you have for me?" "Your voice sounds different. Not using the jeep's radio?' "No, the lobby phone." Then Gladys said," You've been working so hard they're going to give you a helper." "A helper as in an assistant?" "Not exactly. The meeting Mr. Summers was in that caused him to be late for yours and Alanah's appointment was to approve the hiring of another ranger for security, search and rescue. According to forecasts, the park will again break the four million visitor benchmark for this year. The only drawback is, he is fresh out of college with no practical on-the-job training." "Well, I've been told patience is a virtue so guess I better brush up on my people patience skills. Fresh out of college, you say?" "Yes, Sir. Just graduated, Summa Cum Laude." "Thanks for the heads-up Gladys. When will he come on board?" "I believe he is waiting for you now in the lobby. Good luck."

Hanging up the phone, Mike looked around and saw someone in a ranger uniform standing in front of the lobby's window, looking outside. He walked up and when he was about ten feet away the young man turned and saw him. "Mr. Murphy. Gladys said I would find you here. Daniel Snyder. The new guy on the block." Right away Mike liked the young man standing in front of him. His uniform was neatly creased with his name tag and park emblem correctly in place and his ranger hat sitting square on his head."You drink coffee?" Mike asked. "Yes, Sir. Grew to like the taste while in the military." "Good, let's find a seat." As soon as they sat down at a table, a waitress came over and took their order and less than five minutes later she sat down two steaming cups of coffee in front of them along with a few individual creamers on a small dish. "You mentioned military? What branch?" Asked Mike. "Army. Spent three tours in Afghanistan as part of an EOD team. While in the service I took several online courses getting some fundamental requirements out of the way. After an honorable discharge I challenged several courses and received my Masters in Forestry a year early. I wasn't the youngest to receive a degree as that honor goes to Karl Witte, who at the age of thirteen received a Doctorate in Philosophy."

"I understand you graduated Summa Cum Laude. That is quite an honor." "I suppose. My father was a hard taskmaster and being an only son I could never quite match his standards of excellence." "So why a park ranger? You could have had your choice of anything the world has to offer. Your father a businessman?" "Yes, Sir, Mr. Murphy. He owns an aerospace electronics firm and often works directly with NASA. He was very disappointed when I said I wanted to go into forestry as he wanted me to eventually inherit the company but didn't hesitate in paying the full tuition the same day I registered. I like the fresh air and freedom of outdoors and being a park ranger, you can't get much better than that."

The two of them sat and talked over several cups of coffee and finally Mike asked, "You ready to hit the

78

road? Gladys or Louise didn't leave any instructions or bear sightings when I called in this morning so guess we are on our own." "Yes, Sir, Mr. Murphy." "Got to make a short detour to the bathroom first, too much coffee and call me Mike." "Yes, Sir, uh Mike."

The air that morning had a definite chill in it as they walked across the parking lot to where the Wrangler was sitting in its reserved space. "Mr. Murphy, Mike, if we are going to be driving around the park, could I drive with you giving instructions? It would help in getting my orientation and sense of direction in place much quicker." "Sure, good thinking," agreed Mike as he reached into his pocket then tossed the keys to Daniel. "Just take a left out of the lot and we are on our way."

The traffic that morning wasn't bad at all and as Mike sat in the passenger seat he couldn't help but admire the smooth driving skills of Daniel. He always kept both hands on the wheel unless he was shifting gears or making turns and using the directional lever. While driving, his eyes continually shifted from the road directly ahead to things as they passed them on the roadside. Several times that morning, Mike directed Daniel to pull over at campsites and Mike would introduce himself to guests and inquire about bear sightings or if they had observed anything out of the ordinary. Most of the guests said they had not seen any bears, but several mentioned deer and a profusion of red squirrels.

At the Tioga Pass entrance they turned around and headed back. Mike explained the entrance was normally closed west of this point, November to May each year. At Tuolumne Meadows Mike suggested they stop for an early lunch and his suggestion was met with a wide grin from Daniel. "I was thinking of asking about grabbing a snack as coffee is good but doesn't compare to a hamburger and fries." Mike chuckled as he thought about young people and junk food then said, "Don't know about a burger and fries but I'm sure there is something for everyone here." During the meal, Daniel paused with a forkful of food halfway to his mouth, looked across the table at Mike and asked, "Mike, you remember that guest who mentioned seeing a lot of red squirrels?" "Yes, that is normal anytime in the park, especially late in the year as they are stocking away nuts and seeds for the Winter. Why do you ask?" "I was wondering if they were Chickaree or better known as Douglas squirrels?" "Excellent observation and question. Most probably Douglas." "I guess all that money father paid for my education paid off," said Daniel as he grinned and laughed.

The remainder of the orientation tour passed uneventful and late in the afternoon Mike directed Daniel back to the parking lot at the District Office. As they sat in the jeep Mike pointed out the park museum built in 1925 by Herbert Maier which was the first building in the National Park Service specifically built as a museum. "Well, what did you think of the tour of Yosemite?" Asked Mike. "Very impressive. I understand over ninety percent of the park is considered wilderness?" "Correct. You will fit in just fine, Daniel. I usually call in around seven AM to get a heads-up from either Gladys or Louise about the day's schedule, but most of the time they have nothing so I, or we, will be making rounds to various camping facilities or campgrounds, pretty much like today. In the Winter months, or anytime actually there is the possibility of a search and rescue for lost or stranded guests, You'll be staying at The Valley, same as me, so what say we check in, find some dinner and get an early start in the morning?" "Sounds like a game plan, Mike."

The next morning, both Mike and Daniel were asked to help out with traffic control at Valley Visitor Center. At the end of the day Daniel asked, "So this is pretty much what it's like this late in the season or year?" "Pretty much," answered Mike. But this is nothing to compare when Winter hits the park and snow becomes an every item to deal with." "That's okay, Mike, I actually like snow." "Okay, I'll remind you that you said that if we have to go out in the big snow cat when it is twenty degrees and the wind blowing thirty miles an hour."

Chapter Eleven

Winter came and transformed the park into a wonderland of fresh, snow brushed fir trees and deep drifts in the higher elevations. From mid December to early April, Badger Pass is usually closed and vehicles were not permitted between Crane Flat and Tioga Pass due to hazardous conditions. Tire chains were required over many of the park roads. However, Badger Pass Road was plowed and open to the Yosemite ski and snowboarding area. Deep snow was great for skiers, but it also taxed the experts. In open areas, fresh snow was easy to navigate, but when hidden rocks came into play, even the experienced skiers often limped into the lodges with sprained ankles.

As planned, Alanah graduated, Magna Cum Laude and after a week of orientation, officially joined the staff of Yosemite as Public Relations Director. December was already here and the Bracebridge dinner was just a few weeks away. Mike and Daniel were both on call for any emergencies that might come up. Fortunately, bear sightings were minimal as most were in hibernation..

January and February came and went and the park was firmly locked in Winter's grip. The roads around the snowboarding and ski areas were kept plowed. Cross country skiers were in their element and deep snow drifts were no problem. In March things started to thaw and the creeks ran full because of snow melt.

After a long hard Winter, Spring came to Yosemite. Old Man Winter made one last desperate attempt to keep the park encased in snow and ice by bringing a foot of snow to Badger Pass in early April. By mid May only a few patches of snow were left in the higher elevations. Mike was tired, both physically and mentally as both he and Daniel had been called on several occasions, to rescue guests who chose to disregard posted signs about dangerous skiing conditions. No one was seriously injured, but exposure to harsh elements brought its toll in stress and anxiety, even to the most experienced outdoors person.

Alanah had been the hero who saved the day with all her efforts to see that guests enjoyed their stay during the holidays, especially with all the details of the Bracebridge dinner. From December thirteen to Christmas day, eight performances by over a hundred actors, dancers and bards, transform the Ahwahnee into a 17th. century English manor.

The event consists of a seven course dinner over a four hour period; Renaissance ceremonies and music from the middle ages helped to recreate the roles of Squire Bracebridge, his family and the Lord of Misrule. The dinner had been held every year since 1927.

"Mike, you remember what you told me about that bear with the missing claw?" Asked Alanah, as they sat at a table having breakfast. "You mean Molly? The one that we trapped, tagged and released? Yes, why do you ask?" "What became of her?" "Good question Sweetheart. I hadn't thought about it. I could check and see if she still has her tag. Sometimes the tag comes loose if they get into a fight with another bear. When I check in with Louise, before making my rounds, I'll ask if she can locate her." "Thank you. I have some details to work out for a conference coming up in a few days. We can compare notes tonight?" Suggested Alanah. "Works for me," said Mike as they got up from the table, kissed and continued with the day's activities.

After a full season of rescuing lost guests, Mike enjoyed a day of just driving and checking various campsites to make sure they were ready to receive backpackers and campers. That evening, as they again sat across from each other enjoying dinner, Mike said, "Louise checked and Molly still has her ear tag and apparently has come out of hibernation. According to the GPS she is up in the northwestern part of the park, around Rancheria Falls." Alanah sat for a few minutes, poked at her food with a fork, then asked," Could we go see her? I know it sounds silly and it's only one bear." "That area is pretty rugged and only accessible by hiking in. You sure? It would take most of a day, possibly overnight?"

" I'm sure," said Alanah."We haven't been camping out for a while and I think getting away, just the two of us, would be good. You've been cranky, on several occasions and also myself. We need a break." Mike could not but agree with Alanah's reasoning. It had been a rough season and they had not spent much quality time with each other, much like two ships passing in the night. "Want to try for next weekend? I'll clear it with Mr. Summers. We can leave out from Hetch Ketchy Saturday morning?" "Saturday is good. I have that weekend off anyway," agreed Alanah.

The week passed quickly and early Saturday morning Mike parked the Wrangler at Backpacker's campground, then opened the rear compartment and got out their backpacks. He always kept his ready to go at a moment's notice so it was simply a matter of preparing Alana's for the hike the night before. Ten minutes later they were on their way. The morning was slowly warming up and a half hour into the trip they had to take off a layer of clothing. A few times Mike suggested they take a breather. He didn't actually need one, but Alanah was not breathing easily. "A hard day at the office?" he asked jokingly. "It isn't that. I'm just not in as good a shape as you, but I'll manage. How much farther?" She asked. "Maybe another half hour, tops." "Just let me catch my breath. I can see why you love your job so much. Even being so rugged it is beautiful." Almost exactly a half hour later, Mike announced, "According to the GPS, this should be where she was last reported."

Setting his backpack down, Mike reached into a side pocket and got out a pair of field glasses and began scanning the area. Even being as rugged as it was, there was a small meadow about a half mile away. As Mike looked through the binoculars a bear came through some thick bushes at the edge of the clearing, behind the bear were two small cubs. As he watched the bear walk, he noticed a slight limp in her gait. It had to be Molly. He handed the binoculars to Alanah and as she brought the glasses up to her eyes, she let out a sigh and said softly,

"She has two cubs. Oh, Mike, thank you. Coming up

here, I wasn't sure if I could make it, but seeing this, it was well worth falling over a few rocks and getting bruised knees."

Alanah then lowered the binoculars, wiped away a few tears and then again looked at Molly and her cubs as they walked across the clearing and disappeared into the thick underbrush. With her free hand, she reached down and grasped Mike's hand firmly. Finally, she lowered the binoculars, wiped away a few more tears and smiled broadly. Taking a deep breath and slowly letting it out, Alanah said, "It's been a wonderful morning. Thank you. If you are ready, we can head back?" "Seeing Molly and her cubs was worth the climb," Mike said, then added,"A few times I wondered about her because she hadn't been reported as raiding any campgrounds. I guess she lost the taste for human food. It's better for them that way. Yes, if you're up to it, we can head back. This time we take it slow and easy. My treat for dinner tonight."